# *Princess* *Diana*

TEXT BY
**ANN CHUBB**

FEATURING THE
PHOTOGRAPHY OF
**DAVID LEVENSON**

DESIGNED BY
**SARA COOPER**

PRODUCED BY
**TED SMART and
DAVID GIBBON**

COOMBE BOOKS

The photograph of the shy teenager pictured with a toddler on each hip startled the world. She was pretty, yes, in the typical teenage way of autumn 1980, but you would scarcely have given her a second glance on a number eleven bus. Her clothes, too, were the typical teenage clothes of that autumn; practical separates such as a cosy knit pullover teamed with a rather too see-through flower-printed skirt. Was this really the next Queen of England?

It was, and what is more this shy teenager was not only married to the heir to the British throne within a matter of months, she also became a leader of fashion, with her face adorning more magazine covers around the world than any other woman before her.

After the initial shock of those early pictures, the world's heart warmed to the then Lady Diana Spencer. Yes, of course she was just right for the job when you thought about it. "A little young maybe, but why not? And doesn't she look just like..." The best thing about the quickly, and fondly-dubbed 'Lady Di' was that she looked very much like everybody's daughter/girlfriend /girl-next-door. And wasn't it nice that the girl-next-door was going to be Queen?

She was immediately watched and adored by both the nation and the world, who saw her as a future 'princess of the people'. We scrutinized her every move and enjoyed every minute of her rapid rise to fame and riches, as though she were our own daughter. We liked to think it was a real Cinderella story; the sweet little kindergarten teacher in her Laura Ashley skirt, who charmed her Prince and married him, after a whirlwind romance, wearing a fairy-tale wedding dress.

In fact, Lady Diana Spencer was almost royal from the start. Both she and Prince Charles are directly descended from Charles I and she was born on the Sandringham estate. Her grandmother, Lady Fermoy, is lady-in-waiting to the Queen Mother; the Queen is godmother to her younger brother and there are countless other ties with the Royal Family. She had been brought up with them as country neighbours and her sister had had a romance with Prince Charles some years previously. Her life style, far from girl-next-door, was distinctly 'Sloane Ranger' – the name coined for that elite band of well-heeled girls who frequent the Sloane Street/Knightsbridge area.

Her clothes, it was true, did often come from Laura Ashley, just like the girl-next-door's, although that first, famous see-through skirt came from Liberty's Regent Street store and was made of rather pricey Tana lawn – the very best quality.

But to us she was still the People's Princess. We loved the way she discreetly fended off the Press as they hounded her relentlessly in those pre-engagement days. And the Press in turn loved the way she discreetly lowered her eyes below her heavy, sun-streaked fringe in a way that quickly earned her the name of 'Shy Di'.

From the moment that first picture flashed around the world, her every movement was monitored. As our Princess-to-be fled from Mini to doorstep, her every outfit hit the headlines. We loved her frilly blouses, her flat heels and knickerbockers and so did the rag trade, who copied them endlessly.

The Sloane Rangers themselves have named her 'Supersloane' and, indeed, she personifies their ladylike, well-bred knack of putting together a little of what is expected of one (good shoes and real pearls) with a little of what is fun (knickerbockers and Bermuda shorts and ethnic woollies).

Her influence was immediate among the Sloane set, who cropped their lanky locks to the same bouncy, heavy-fringed cut, and pronounced "Di-lights" as perfectly O.K. and quite different from common, bleached locks, which would never do.

She was already a style setter; the sort of young style setter we had lacked. She obviously enjoyed clothes, adored shopping and positively glowed as the cameras clicked away at each fashion success.

The British fashion industry glowed, too. Here, at last, was the fashion leader they had longed for. Her frilly blouses were mass-produced by the million. And that spring the young designers who hoped to catch her custom started work on the next autumn's collections with enthusiasm, emerging with the sort of Little Lord Fauntleroy looks that they imagined might tempt her. Every collection featured black velvet knickerbockers and frothy, white lace collars, and the inspiration was obvious.

But could – would – should a sweet, naive nineteen year old take on the responsibility of becoming a future Queen of England? Obviously it wasn't a question that could be rushed and Lady Diana was secretly dispatched to Australia to think it all over with the help of her mother.

When the engagement was announced on February 24th, the world rejoiced, and that afternoon the first official picture of the Royal Couple was released; a picture that was to embellish commemorative stamps, mugs and a million souvenirs the world over.

For a girl so obviously interested in fashion it was strange that Diana took so little time to select an engagement outfit; especially an outfit to be engraved forever on everything from stamps to biscuit boxes. Was it that the engagement announcement was rushed in the end, possibly due to Press pressure? The story goes that Lady Diana simply nipped into Harrods that morning and bought the blue Cojana suit, with its co-ordinating blouse, then and there.

It was to be one of her few big fashion blunders. The blue, it was true, was beautiful – exactly the colour of her eyes and her sapphire ring – with just the right sort of zingy shade. It was, however, sad that it didn't really fit and simply bunched in at her belted waist in rather sack-like fashion.

Perhaps it was the shock of seeing these pictures reproduced so many times that drove Lady Diana straight into the arms of *Vogue*. Months before she had been photographed for them by Lord Snowdon and had much admired the beautiful Emanuel blouse they chose for her to wear. Her sister had worked at *Vogue*, too, so it was far from unfamiliar territory. It was as though, from the moment of that engagement picture, she made a big vow to do better as far as clothes were concerned. Style setter she might be, but suddenly there was a need for the sort of decidedly dressy clothes that she had never worn before. She then and there sought out the very best experts in their field to help her.

Who better than Anna Harvey, a senior *Vogue* fashion editor. Anna, like all fashion editors, is constantly in touch with fashion designers, manufacturers and retailers, and was able to provide Diana with all she needed to know about fashion trends and resources. She has an office wardrobe full of samples of next season's clothes awaiting photography. Who better to go to than her, to try on clothes in privacy without the commitment but with professional and unbiased advice, instead of trekking around the West End and Knightsbridge.

Then there was the question of her hair; no criticisms here so no change either. It was Keith Shanley of Headlines, the South Kensington salon to which Diana had been introduced by her sister, who created that famous Lady Di cut and its "Di-lights".

Make-up was another matter. Diana had seen from her *Vogue* photo session how a professional make-up artist could work magic for the camera, and very natural-looking magic at that. So *Vogue* introduced her to top visagist Barbara Daly.

And it was memories of that *Vogue* session and that romantic-looking blouse that took Lady Diana to the Emanuels' tiny Brook Street salon. Unused to the mystique of couture dressing, she must have been relieved to discover a nice, natural couple not far removed from her own age; David was then 28 years old, Elizabeth 27.

At that point the Emanuels were virtually unknown to the world at large, although anyone who had seen their final-year show when they graduated from the Royal College of Art three years before, knew they were a talent to watch. David, one of eleven sons of a Welsh ex-steelworker, met and married Elizabeth while they were still students at Harrow School of Art and together they went on to the Royal College of Art – the first married couple to do so.

The acclaim they won there convinced Liz's millionaire father that they were worth setting up with a business of their own in Mayfair's Brook Street, and they soon became the darlings of the Society set, attracting clients such as Bianca Jagger and Princess Michael of Kent.

They first designed a couple of ballgowns for Lady Diana. Theirs, for instance, was the spectacular, strapless ballgown of black silk taffeta decorated with diamonte that she wore to the Royal Opera House's gala at Goldsmiths Hall. Here our shy Di was transformed into a positive siren, with totally bare shoulders, and in black, too, a colour rarely worn by royalty.

It was certainly a personal success; a dramatic change of style, too. It showed her stamp of individuality and was a break with tradition. And, what is more, the world saw by his adoring eyes that Charles loved her in it. His little Sloane Ranger was becoming something of a show stopper. The next morning, while the Press tried frantically to track down the rather unexpected choice of designers, Diana rang to thank the Emanuels and report total success. By lunchtime they had some even more exciting news to celebrate. A telephone call from the Palace told them that an announcement was to be made later in the day to the effect that they would be designing the royal wedding dress. By a strange quirk of fate I was lunching with the Emanuels' P.R. at the moment the call came through. She was discretion itself, but not much journalistic intuition was needed to interpret her excited expression. By the time the news went out to the world via the Press Association at four that afternoon, the story was already ready and waiting.

The choice of the Emanuels seemed a good, if unexpected, one. The total break with tradition was what we were beginning to expect from our Princess-to-be. Instead of trailing the well-worn path to Hartnell or Amies, the Queen's own dressmakers, or even to someone as well-known as Zandra Rhodes, she was already creating a style of her own. And David Emanuel's totally Welsh background was a diplomatic move by the next Princess of Wales. But as far as Lady Diana was concerned she probably went to them because she admired their young style and fantasy wedding dresses, and because they had proved that they understood what she wanted, as well as being nearer to her age than any of the establishment dressmakers, which made her feel more at ease.

For some brides-to-be, the engagement, however short, can be a miserable time; all worries, plans and discussions with two (or in Diana's case, three) sets of parents to appease, too. But for Diana it was obviously the time of her life. She adored shopping and suddenly she was on the shopping spree of a lifetime. She would drop off at the Emanuels' for fittings, then flit up the adjacent South Molton Street in search of pretty shoes and off-duty separates.

Her mother, meanwhile, whisked her off to Bellville Sassoon for more fittings – for it was they who were making her going-away outfit, among other things – and to John Boyd's little Brompton Arcade shop for hats.

There was Ascot to go to for the first time and, of course, a wedding list to prepare.

Until then, when Diana needed to wear a hat she would simply borrow a masculine trilby from her sister; and suddenly every teenager was wearing such a hat. But something rather more dressy was needed by the time she became engaged, so Diana was taken by her mother to see milliner John

Boyd in his tiny hat shop, just off Knightsbridge. John Boyd was no stranger to Diana – he had long made hats for her mother and still refers to Diana as the "wee lassie". Neither was John a stranger to royalty; he makes hats for Princess Anne among other members of the Royal Family, and also for Margaret Thatcher. Step inside his shop and you will find one wall decorated with nothing but hats – hats so closely associated with their famous wearers that it's almost eerie to see them hanging there. The hats that John Boyd makes for Diana are not so very different from those he makes for anyone else, whether they are famous or not. It's simply the way Diana wears them, casually atop her very young-looking, shaggy haircut – and very much in her own style – that makes them different.

Sometimes John Boyd despairs when he sees his precious hats worn the wrong way round or back-to-front, but really he loves every minute of it and tries hard to give Diana exactly what she wants. He finds fabrics long since out of production for her, so that she can have something really exclusive; hand dyes the veiling to match her outfits, and has found some old-fashioned hairpins in an effort to keep her hats firmly in place whatever the weather conditions.

One of Diana's very first Boyd hats was veiled, and it met with such success that veils have featured prominently in her hat wardrobe ever since. And John Boyd has a clever way of dyeing the veiling so that it is flatteringly darker over the eye area. In fact, visit John Boyd just before a big royal occasion and you are sure to see a colour swatch of Diana's outfit pinned to his tie. It's there so that he can concentrate on dyeing both hat and trimmings to match it exactly; and often his hands, too, will be tinged by the dye bath that he uses.

Not since Jackie Kennedy's heyday have we seen so many pillboxes, while feathered plumes have become as much a hallmark of a Diana hat as her veiling.

Until Diana appeared with her plumes and pillboxes and veiling, the young simply weren't interested in hats, except perhaps if they were casual trilbies like her's. Now it's a very different story. Diana-style hats have been the headliners at Royal Ascot for the past two seasons, and the British millinery industry, long in the doldrums, is reaping the rewards.

Diana remained in the public eye right until the wedding day. The stress only finally began to tell at a June polo match when she rushed off the field in tears, upset by the over-enthusiasm of Fleet Street. Diana, and all the people involved in the wedding preparations, were determined that none of the excitement of the 'wedding of the century' would be diluted by leaks. And the biggest secret of all was the design of the wedding dress – to be guarded at all costs.

The Emanuels were besieged. A television crew was parked permanently outside their Mayfair salon and photographers with telephoto lenses parked themselves in offices opposite, forcing the couple to work continually behind shuttered windows despite the summer heat. Complicated plans were laid to foil possible espionage. Scraps of white fabric were left in the dustbins, while those fabrics pertaining to the dress itself never left the salon. A vast safe was purchased to contain the dress. And, as a final ploy, the Emanuels spread a story that six dresses were being made, and that Diana wouldn't decide until the last minute which one she would wear.

It was decided by the Palace that details of the wedding dress, the bridesmaids' dresses and the pageboy outfits would be released from the Press Centre at seven a.m. on the day of the wedding. As I approached the Press Centre in Shoe Lane (just off Fleet Street) at around six that morning, the roads were already closed, with barricades across them, but one mention of my mission and the barriers were lifted and I drove through.

The sketch that I received that morning was everything that had been expected of it, yet more. It was very Emanuel, very regal and yet as fairy-tale as David Emanuel had predicted it would be.

It was to prove to be a dress, too, that brides the world over chose to wear themselves if they were marrying that year, thanks to the thousands of copies turned out by the bridal wear firms. Within hours of the wedding, the crowds trailing back along the wedding route from St Paul's were able to see the first of those replicas on display in the windows of the Daily Telegraph. Made by Ellis Gowns, one of the largest bridal wear manufacturers, it was to be the first of the many.

But neither the cameras nor the manufacturers could actually capture the intricate and very special detail of that fabulous dress. The fabric, for instance, was specially spun and woven at England's only silk farm – Lullingstone. And it was an ultra heavy weight of ivory taffeta designed to defy creases – the first time such a weight had been attempted.

The trimming of Honiton lace was re-embroidered with thousands of tiny, mother-of-pearl sequins to glint under the lights of the Cathedral, and in order to preserve secrecy, Elizabeth Emanuel and her mother had sat up night after night embroidering it themselves. They had even embroidered a tiny daffodil, to symbolize Wales, onto the potpourri on the dress hanger.

And when the bride emerged, with her dress a little creased, from her carriage, it was evident that her wonderful, twenty-five-foot train had been designed to match the spectacular aisle of St Paul's. The veil, almost as dramatic, was held in place by the Spencer family diamond tiara, and matched by diamond earrings borrowed from her mother. Still in view was that famous fringe. Barely seen, however, were the matching ivory silk slippers made by Clive Shilton. With delicate, half-inch Louis heels and spangled with tiny pearls and mother-of-pearl sequins, they had a frilled, heart-shaped rosette of embroidered and sequined lace.

The enormous, shower-style bouquet was made in the early hours of that day by Doris Wellhan, head florist at Longmans' Fenchurch Street branch, and followed a white and gold theme. Yellow Earl Mountbatten roses were mixed with cream gardenias, white orchids with yellow eyes, white stephanotis, lilies of the valley and freesias. A traditional touch was the inclusion of sprigs of myrtle and veronica from bushes grown from cuttings of Queen Victoria's wedding bouquet.

The Emanuels like to plan every aspect of the wedding 'picture'. Theirs, of course, were the enchanting bridesmaids' dresses, as was the idea of putting circlets of fresh flowers in their hair, and the suggestion of flower baskets instead of posies.

The going-away outfit by Bellville Sassoon aroused far less comment. In coral-pink silk, it had a short, bolero jacket with frilly, organdie collar and cuffs and a slim, side-slit skirt. It was matched with a slightly Edwardian-style tricorn hat with plumes by John Boyd. While the multi-strand pearl choker that the Princess literally borrowed straight from her sister's neck was immediately copied by the million.

Even on the first day of her honeymoon, Diana couldn't forget entirely about fashion. The telephone rang the very next morning at the Emanuels' showroom and a shy voice asked if David or Elizabeth were available. On hearing that they were not, the voice continued, "It's their bride. And I just wanted to thank them for making my day so wonderful."

While the bride was obviously more than happy with the dress of a lifetime, the Press were not so sure. And they certainly didn't like the way that the Emanuels had signed on super-agent Mark McCormack – the entrepreneur who handles franchise deals for the stars. It was reported that he was getting them to charge vast sums for interviews and personal appearances. And that very week a range of Emanuel sunglasses appeared in the shops, to be followed shortly by hosiery, perfume and bed linen. The very afternoon of the wedding, the Emanuels called a Press conference and the feeling was rife that they might be capitalising on the royal event.

In fact, it was Liz's father who had insisted on the appointment of McCormack. As their financial backer, he could see how they were already inundated with offers of all kinds and felt that they needed someone to handle that side of things. The Press thought that this was exploitation, although McCormack's clients already included Mark Phillips. And while Diana's affection for the couple did seem to cool for some time, she has returned to them for "quite a few" dresses during 1983.

A protracted honeymoon, both aboard the Royal Yacht in the Mediterranean and later at Balmoral, meant that little of the Princess was seen for the rest of the summer apart from a lovely, informal picture session in Scotland.

She had barely begun her public engagements when it was announced that she was pregnant. The Royal Couple's delight was obvious, but it was not to be all plain sailing for Diana. She suffered terribly with morning sickness in the initial months, although she bravely attempted to carry on with her commitments. And Press intrusion reached such a pitch that the Queen took the unprecedented step of asking Fleet Street's editors to leave her daughter-in-law in peace, at least for the time being. A step no doubt instigated by the pictures published of an obviously pregnant Princess sunbathing in a bikini on holiday.

Nevertheless, Diana, in her colourful maternity wardrobe, continued to set trends. Her appearance on the polo field in an enormous hand-knitted sweater embellished with a koala bear motif was the most memorable. And as the pregnancy progressed she blossomed forth, first in colourful mohair coats, then in maternity dresses proper, but always with her, by now, signature details – the pretty collars, the chokers and necklaces of pearls – all ideal accessories to distract from increasing bulk and to play up a blooming complexion. And she insisted on visiting Ascot just days before the expected birth. Strange to think that less than twenty years ago pregnant royalty were seldom seen in public at all!

After the birth of Prince William, Diana matured quickly. Her evident love of children must have made this the pinnacle of her happiness. Before her marriage, children had been her career – she taught at the Young London Kindergarten – and time and time again she has proved that she is never happier or more relaxed than when she has a baby to hold and cuddle, whether her own or someone else's. Maybe that is why 'Shy Di', as she was, chose to be pictured with a toddler on each hip when she posed officially for the Press for the very first time.

She's obviously a natural mother, and it was with great aplomb that she quietened her crying baby at his Christening, despite the presence of the world's cameras.

The fulfilment of her desire to become a mother, and her obvious pride in motherhood, helped her enormously in overcoming much of her early shyness, and gave her a new confidence. And she certainly needed it, for she was quickly plunged back into the swing of royal duties after the birth, and at two sad occasions. There was the Falklands Memorial Service, for instance, and soon after that she flew alone to Monaco to represent the Queen at the funeral of Princess Grace.

While it's quite clear that Charles and Diana would love to add to their family as soon as possible, their hectic schedule of public tours and endless engagements, both at home and abroad, may have delayed their plans a little longer than hoped for, although their mutual desire ultimately to have a large family is well known.

Figures don't just pop back into shape after a birth as most young mothers discover with dismay! And when the world's cameras are focusing on your girth within days of the event, it must be particularly distressing. Diana very wisely chose a loose maternity dress for her hospital departure, instead of something new. William was, after all, less than a week old. But this was hardly the sort of outfit she could wear for the Falklands Memorial Service just a few weeks later. Maybe it was those rather more revealing pictures of her in her windblown, blue silk dress that sparked off a bout of dieting that was so drastic that it was rumoured that she was suffering from the slimmers' disease, anorexia nervosa. Suddenly, the prettily plump teenager of the engagement days, who had always been a good size twelve, and the comely bride who quickly became pregnant, was becoming thinner by the minute. She publicly picked at her food at official functions and her once full face developed the bony look of model girls'.

In all probability, Diana's love of fashion had a lot to do with her new slimness. She, more than anyone, must have been aware of how much better her clothes looked in the pictures taken in the days immediately following the wedding when, as with most brides, she had lost a little weight. She must have realised, too, the enormous impact that her clothes were making world-wide, and she became increasingly aware that this was an area where she could do much to help influence British fashion, and in a way that she enjoyed.

For most of the first nine months of marriage she had had to restrict her wardrobe to maternity clothes. The autumn of 1982 was the first time that she could really indulge her passion for fashion in a big way, and she meant to do it properly.

She was becoming increasingly dependent on *Vogue,* too, although her designers all agree that, when it comes down to it, she has very definite views of her own. It was in the December of 1982 that she attended her very first fashion show; a grand evening 'do' at the Guildhall. It had been arranged by *Vogue's* Anna Harvey for 'Birthright' – a charity close to the Princess' heart, and one with which her own gynaecologist, George Pinker, was deeply involved, too.

The theme of the fashion show was 'party dressing' and both show and audience strongly featured the big evening wear trend of that winter – the masculine, black dinner suit, worn complete with wing-collared shirt and bow tie. Diana, probably wishing to be distinctly different, stole the evening in her stunning, one-shouldered dress of brilliant blue silk with its black, coin dot print. Designed by Bruce Oldfield, it was softer and slimmer than her usual evening look and she stood out brilliantly against everyone else's black. She had done it again! The switch to a softer, slimline silhouette made everyone else look decidedly dated! And the one-shouldered look that she launched that evening has since taken off in a big way.

It became obvious that, far from remaining with the fairy-tale looks of bouffant ball gowns and frilly collars that had so entranced us initially, she was continually experimenting with different styles and broadening her stable of designers in a constant search for a unique look that was hers and hers alone.

There was no attempt to be loyal to the longtime royal favourites such as Hardy Amies and the House of Hartnell. Bellville Sassoon was probably her only predictable choice and one that suits her very well. She visited them early on in her engagement days and they have proved adept at providing just the right outfit, whether for day or night. While some of the Princess' most ravishing evening outfits have come from this house, they were also responsible for her much-copied sailor suit of engagement days.

Bruce Oldfield is a more daring choice by far. Tall, handsome and coloured, he's an ex-student of St Martin's College of Art, best known for the sexy, glamourous gowns he has designed for the likes of Joan Collins and Charlotte Rampling.

Understandably, Diana has often chosen designers of an age close to her own. Arabella Pollen, for instance, at just 21 herself, never makes the Princess look older than her years. The darling of the Sloane Ranger set, she also bears a striking resemblance to the Princess. Hers, for instance, was the much-photographed suit of pale, banana-yellow tweed, with its double-breasted jacket and brown velvet collar.

Certainly it must be far less difficult for a young girl to relate to a designer of her own age than to visit some very grand and daunting salon.

Jasper Conran, also 21, is another favourite with Diana – his are the rather severe, tailored slimline suits she's worn recently and which suit her so well, also making a big break with her previous, rather fussy, daywear.

Diana quite obviously has a passion for shops; whether it's a visit to the local sweet shops near Highgrove, or a quick recce to South Molton Street to find out what's new in London's world of fashion.

Perhaps, when she's immersed in the hunt for a new pair of shorts or shoes, Diana feels nearest to the girl in the street that she was until not so long ago. And the impromptu nature of her shopping trips means that she is often treated far more naturally, without any of the pomp and ceremony that have now become a regular part of her life.

She walked into the knitwear specialist shop Tomlinsons, just off Kensington High Street, quite unexpectedly recently. The staff were so taken aback that they treated her just as they would a normal customer, and that is probably what she wanted. Her purchase was a hand-knitted cardigan with a cheerful, rainbow motif knitted across its back.

South Molton Street became a favourite shopping beat with the Princess when she was visiting the Emanuels for her wedding dress fittings. Their salon is almost on its southerly corner, so once she was parked she could swoop in on the maximum number of fashionable shops in the minimum time. Not only does it have a good selection of high fashion merchants (Browns, Joseph, Kenzo, Benetton, plus all the best shoe chains), it's strictly pedestrians only, so that it can be encompassed in a matter of minutes.

Sloane Rangers are so named because of their love of the Sloane Street/Knightsbridge area, which has been named as their 'natural habitat'. Diana is no exception. Harvey Nichols is her favourite store and, before it became generally known that she frequented it, she would often meet girl-friends for lunch at Harveys, their top floor restaurant. Just behind Harvey Nichols is Laura Ashley – a favourite from her pre-engagement days. It's handy too for Bellville Sassoon, just across Sloane Street in Pavilion Road. Then there's Harrods, of course. Slip out of the back door and you're almost in Beauchamp Place, where Bruce Oldfield is to be found. Caroline Charles – another favourite – is there too, and Diana goes to both personally for fittings.

Not far away, in Pimlico's Elizabeth Street, is the little Inca Shop, and Diana's love of their cheap and colourful Peruvian sweaters has kept the peasants at home happily clicking away at the knitting needles for some time now. For, while Diana constantly flies the flag for British fashion in her public appearances, she obviously loves a touch of the ethnic, which creeps in here and there, especially on more casual occasions. On the polo field, for instance, she is hardly ever without one of those useful, quilted bags in Provencal printed cotton which she buys at Soleido in the Fulham Road. It has been said that she also secretly buys from Kenzo, and certainly this Paris based Japanese designer with a shop in Sloane Street has the clothes that suit her well, but she's far too discreet to wear them in public.

By the time Charles and Diana ended their first overseas tour (to Australia and New Zealand, in April 1983), it was obvious that Diana had been shopping for the best of British fashion in a big way. No less than fifty outfits were reported to have been worn over the 42 days of the tour. On most days, at least three changes were needed to cover a wide diversity of events, not to mention weather. Certain favourite outfits from the past reappeared, like the coral-pink going-away outfit and the scarlet jerkin suit with its red and white striped blouse. But critics of the Princess' high expenditure shouldn't forget that she had had absolutely no wardrobe to speak of before her engagement, just over two years before, and had spent most of the first year pregnant. She owned very few high summer outfits, for instance, and certainly not nearly enough to cover the demanding six weeks of the tour. Nor did she have enough of the grand evening gowns that the world would expect her to be seen in. Hats, however, she did own in abundance and John Boyd turned his whole workroom over to steaming, refurbishing and re-trimming many of her old ones as well as creating new ones in the weeks leading up to the beginning of the tour.

She widened her net still further in her search for a variety of suitable clothes. Many of her labels may have a very un-British ring about them but, in fact, they are all designers who work for British companies.

Jan Vanvelden, whose pretty, silk outfits with their serrated collars, which were seen so much in Australia and New Zealand, is in fact Dutch born. He worked as a designer for the firm of Salvador for many years and has had his own company here for about two seasons.

Benny Ong comes from Singapore and, as well as a designer collection has a cheaper cotton collection made back home. It was from this that the Princess chose the white cotton separates that she wore to climb Ayers Rock.

And while she buys many outfits like these off-the-peg because she is a standard size, she often has to have them lengthened. Benny lengthened skirts especially for her, for not only is she taller than average, she also prefers longer hemlines. They enable her to bend her legs a little in pictures, disguising the fact that she is as tall as Charles.

Victor Edelstein is no stranger to royalty and counts Princess Michael of Kent among his impressive list of clients. Diana ordered two rose-pink outfits from him for Australia – one was the silk chiffon dress with bows on the shoulders that she wore for a reception in Brisbane.

From Murray Arbeid there was the pale yellow taffeta ballgown that she wore to the dinner given by the Governor General in Canberra. Murray shares a shop in Sloane Street with the Queen's milliner Frederick Fox, who Diana, in her attempts to break new ground, hasn't visited so far.

Frenchman Roland Klein is another of Diana's favourites. She first saw his clothes in his shop immediately beneath the Emanuels' showroom and in Harvey Nichols. Now he, too, supplies her through *Vogue* with dresses, like the strapless ballgown with the checked taffeta skirt.

But the most stunning outfit of all in Australia was the one-shouldered dress of silver and white that she wore for her last night in Melbourne. Hachi, who designed it, is Japanese born, but again London based for several years. In the summer of '81 he almost severed his right hand on a glass bowl and it was saved by microsurgery; so for him that dress represents a very special triumph.

But while Diana flies the flag for the British fashion industry in a way no member of the Royal Family has ever done, she has developed a definite liking for French shoes. While her fixation for 'flatties' is famous and has done much to help the British shoe trade (Clarks factory in Somerset took on extra workers to help produce enough Diana-style pumps), her own come from Charles Jourdan in Knightsbridge. For someone who spends as much time on her feet as Diana, comfortable shoes are all important, and she has discovered that the famous French last suits her feet well.

Johnny Gardner, the stylish ex-model who runs the wholesale side of Jourdan in this country, and who looks after Diana personally, is jokingly known as the "royal footman". When the Princess scuffed her slippers in Australia it was he who urgently dispatched spares. And when he was recently confined to the London Clinic with a back problem, the Princess wrote personally to wish him well.

So the otherwise depressing news bulletins of the spring and early summer were enlivened by six weeks of Diana on the Royal Tour of Australasia doing her one-girl fashion show in a seemingly endless wardrobe. Here she was on walkabouts by day, often bareheaded and barelegged, obviously trying hard to fit in with the more casual mood of the country. And while she made an obvious attempt to foil critics of her high expenditure on clothes by wearing some outfits that dated as far back as her pre-wedding days, the new outfits were stunners. It was becoming clear that her taste in clothes was growing up, with far fewer of those girlish frills. Instead, there were lots of soft, silk dresses by day, and by night there were those stunning new evening dresses – again far more grown-up and elegant. There was the wonderful, wasp-waisted and intricately stitched yellow taffeta dress by Murray Arbeid that she wore to dinner at Government House, Canberra. There was the rose-pink silk ballgown with its tucked bodice of flat pleats and flattering shoulder bows by Victor Edelstein. And finally there was that sensational one-shouldered dress of sparkling embroidered and beaded silk by Hachi. This dress appeared on the last night of the Australian tour and looked as though it might have been worn as one in the eye for the Australian fashion press, who had rather bitchily described the Princess' clothes as "dowdy". Did they really expect to see the future Queen of England dressed like a pop star?

But that Hachi dress certainly silenced them. They had asked for a sexy Princess and here she was. Not only had the Princess proved herself the best possible ambassadress of British fashion, she had proved herself a superb representative of the Queen and the country, and all on her very first overseas tour.

She noticeably outshone her born-to-the-job husband in a way he patently adored. Her natural warmth and spontaneous charm added a new dimension to an already popular Prince. And mothers the world over admired her tenacity in overcoming royal protocol by insisting that she take her baby with her rather than be parted from him for a whole six weeks. It was a move that added a very human and domesticated touch to the tour and set the seal on its success.

After a short break, the Royal Couple set out for their tour of Canada, but this time without William. Diana's new-found confidence, boosted by her successes in Australia and New Zealand, was evident. She was obviously enjoying her new role as ambassadress of fashion. Her taste in clothes was becoming very much more confident – less frills and more of those sleek, tailored suits she wears so well. Her look is maturing fast, with a more sophisticated use of colour (lots of black and white, for instance) and many more figure-hugging evening dresses.

Ever since Charles gave Diana a sapphire the colour of her eyes for her engagement ring, her jewellery has proved as style-setting as her clothes. Within weeks of the engagement pictures, cheap copies of that huge sapphire surrounded by diamonds were already mass-produced and on sale at the chain stores. So was the multi-strand choker of pearls that Diana borrowed from her sister on the wedding day itself to wear with her going-away outfit.

Not since Queen Mary's days have pearls been so popular. And not simply those multi-strand chokers that are such favourites with Diana, but also the simpler strands that she wears.

As a Sloane Ranger, Diana's jewellery was modest and minimal, although the Spencer family did have a treasure chest available for special occasions, and it was the family tiara that Diana chose for her wedding day and which she has often been seen wearing since for official functions.

When she first wore her emerald green taffeta ballgown (for an early Snowdon portrait before her marriage) the emeralds were on loan from the Mayfair jewellers Collingwoods – but now she has a handsome set of her own with matching earrings.

Since the wedding, Diana's own personal collection of jewels has grown appreciably. There are the famous sapphires, for instance, that were a wedding present from the Saudi Royal Family – a huge sapphire pendant on a diamond necklace with matching earrings and bracelet.

Then there is Queen Mary's diamond tiara with its lovers' knots and dangling pearls that was a present from the Queen. The impressive sunray necklace of diamonds that Diana often wears is also from Queen Mary's collection, and it seems that Diana has a similar taste in jewels.

It is rumoured too, that the Duchess of Windsor has a fine collection of royal gems which she intends to bequeath to her great-nephew, Charles.

So far, Diana's most worn pieces are probably her very special earrings – the sapphires surrounded by diamonds, which convert quickly to rubies surrounded by diamonds – and she wears them with a casual cardigan as often as she does with a ballgown.

While much has been written about Diana's favourite designers, very little has been made of the fact that there are some notable omissions. While she has, perhaps understandably, totally ignored the traditional and rather daunting couture houses patronised by the older royals, and deliberately set out to cultivate far younger, and often relatively unknown designers, there are some surprising exceptions.

Zandra Rhodes, for instance, was among those designers tipped to create the wedding dress and she could have done it beautifully. Zandra has designed lovely dresses for Princess Anne, and her exquisitely embroidered and beaded silk chiffons would suit Diana admirably. But Zandra is a very strong and dominant personality, with her flaming pink hair and flamboyant make-up, and perhaps she was just a bit more than a very new Princess (especially a Princess-to-be) felt she could cope with.

Then there was Bill Gibb – the quiet, well-loved Scottish genius who is as clever at creating intricately patterned and coloured knitwear as he is at producing the most exotic creations in leather or lace. But Bill's style is a sophisticated one and maybe it's a look that Diana feels she may well grow into wearing in the future.

She hasn't visited Jean Muir's Bruton Street showroom either, although it's possible that she has bought her clothes off-the-peg at Harvey Nichols, where she still shops regularly. Again, maybe she feels these are sophisticated clothes that she has plenty of time to get around to later on.

And why nothing from the collection of Sheridan Barnett? His pure, clean, uncluttered lines look particularly good on tall girls. And what about Margaret Howell's terribly British, tailored suits – a great favourite with the *Vogue* girls who not only feature them in the magazine, but also choose to wear them.

And, most curious of all, why no hats by the bearded Australian milliner, Freddie Fox, who makes most of the Queen's hats, and very beautifully too. It's especially surprising because Freddie shares both a Sloane Square shop and a Bond Street showroom with Murray Arbeid, who is one of the Princess' latest finds. The charming Freddie, with his twinkling blue eyes, is a constant visitor to Balmoral so surely can be no stranger to Diana?

It looks as though Diana's style is going to have as big an influence on childrens' clothes manufacturers as it has had on the fashion trade. Already, mothers all over the world are discarding easy-care, drip-dry baby suits in stretch fabrics in favour of hand-smocked silk romper suits just like Prince William's. Never mind the ironing, it's the look that counts, and just how fashionable this look has quickly become can be judged from the fact that one Derbyshire factory producing such garments has recently reopened due to renewed demand.

The Italians, too, long considered to be trend-setters when it comes to childrens' wear fashion, have decreed that Bond Street-style sailor suits will be the look of the future for tiny tots.

Not only is it one of Diana's favourite fashion looks, it's a strong theme at Bond Street's White House, where the Royal tots are traditionally dressed, and it seems that William is no exception. So far he has continued to follow their up-market, traditional style, so we can expect to see him wearing navy blue and white cotton sailor suits (especially for parties), silk buster suits and velvet collared wool coats – white flannel for summer, navy blue tweed for winter.

Diana's success as a fashion ambassadress was best reflected by the huge numbers of international buyers who descended on London for the London fashion week. Not since the 'Swinging Sixties' had there been such a buzz of excitement in the fashion world. The Americans in particular had decided that, thanks to our Princess of Wales, London was suddenly where it was all at, fashionwise. *Womans Wear Daily,* the bible of the American fashion world, sent no less than their Editor-in-Chief to find out what was going on and he declared the city was "directional" and had a "passion for fashion". All the top American stores came to look, too, including Bendels, Saks Fifth Avenue, Berdgorf Goodman and Macy's. Not only did they come, they raved and they bought, went off to Paris for the collections then came back and bought again. And it was to the Princess' favourite designers that they headed first – particularly Jasper Conran, Arabella Pollen and Jan Vanvelden. There was a huge interest too in Hachi who, unlike the rest, didn't have a show at all but was inundated with buyers who searched him out in his workrooms just off Bond Street.

The designers responded with a splendid party at Sotheby's. Then the whole British fashion industry celebrated with a grand fashion ball at Grosvenor House presided over by Anna Harvey who, together with Princess Michael of Kent, judged a fashion competition to find the best clothes. And the Emanuels launched two brand-new wholesale collections of mass-produced clothes with a lavish fashion show at the London Branch of Maxims, showing how anyone could dress like a princess for as little as £80.

But it wasn't simply the Princess' designers who sold clothes and celebrated. The rub-off was beneficial to the whole industry. The international visitors were as interested in street fashion as they were in ballgowns. They trekked out to Camden Palace to watch street fashion in its night-time habitat, then sought out these brand-new struggling talents at exhibitions and market stalls.

For days, the London fashion trade was kept so busy writing orders that it was impossible to contact anybody.

In fact, our fashion industry, in the doldrums since the Sixties, seems set to benefit for a long time to come from our style-setting and fashionable Princess.

The Princess of Wales' hats are already legendary and have injected new life into the British millinery industry, for so long in the doldrums until Diana came on the scene. Diana had to wear hats for all her many formal engagements and went along to John Boyd's Knightsbridge salon, where both her mother and Margaret Thatcher buy their hats. John Boyd has known Diana since she was a little girl and still refers to her as "the wee lassie". In fact, the hats he makes for Diana aren't very different from those he makes for anyone else (Princess Anne shops there too); it's simply the way Diana wears them so irreverently atop her sunstreaked shaggy bob of hair, sometimes (to John Boyd's horror) perching them not at all in the way he intended. She gave them a totally different and very young slant. As a result, it is difficult to attend any social event without encountering umpteen "Diana" hats – veiled, plumed or side-tipped, and often all three at once.

The Princess of Wales' hats are already legendary and have injected new life into the British millinery industry, for so long in the doldrums until Diana came on the scene. Diana had to wear hats for all her many formal engagements and went along to John Boyd's Knightsbridge salon, where both her mother and Margaret Thatcher buy their hats. John Boyd has known Diana since she was a little girl and still refers to her as "the wee lassie". In fact, the hats he makes for Diana aren't very different from those he makes for anyone else (Princess Anne shops there too); it's simply the way Diana wears them so irreverently atop her sunstreaked shaggy bob of hair, sometimes (to John Boyd's horror) perching them not at all in the way he intended. She gave them a totally different and very young slant. As a result, it is difficult to attend any social event without encountering umpteen "Diana" hats – veiled, plumed or side-tipped, and often all three at once.

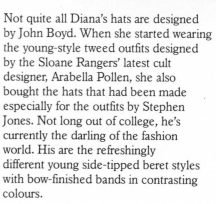

Not quite all Diana's hats are designed by John Boyd. When she started wearing the young-style tweed outfits designed by the Sloane Rangers' latest cult designer, Arabella Pollen, she also bought the hats that had been made especially for the outfits by Stephen Jones. Not long out of college, he's currently the darling of the fashion world. His are the refreshingly different young side-tipped beret styles with bow-finished bands in contrasting colours.

One of the very first formal hats that Diana wore while she was still Lady Diana, was a veiled one. Prince Charles is reported to have loved it, and ever since then veiled styles have been something of a Diana signature, whether or not the veil covers her face, her eyes or simply forms a flamboyant bow trim. When the veil actually covers her face, John Boyd very often dyes the veiling so that it is paler over the skin than on the eyes. And critics of Her Highness' high expenditure should note that not only do the same hats reappear on several occasions, as here, but are often retrimmed to match newer outfits.

Veiled hats are now as much a Diana hallmark as are her ruffled collars, pearl necklaces and chokers, which are often worn with them. Always fastidious about colour co-ordination, John Boyd scores here because, upstairs, above his tiny Brompton Arcade shop, he hand-dyes not only the veiling, so that it matches exactly, but all the other trims too, such as the feathered plumes that Diana herself is particularly fond of. Sample swatches of the colours he is currently working on are often pinned on his tie while his hands are frequently multi-hued from the dye bath.

Until Diana's appearance on the Royal scene in her typical young Sloane Ranger uniform, the Sloanes were something of an elitist clan. Diana not only typified the Sloanes at their best, she added a certain style of her own that both the Press and the rag trade loved. Sloane style was instantly copied and available up and down every high street – even the chain stores had copies of the Sloanes' favourite green "huskies". Until Diana's arrival on the scene, Sloanes all wore their hair long and straight, very probably in a black velvet Alice band too. Now bobs and fringes just like hers are the thing, while those highlights that look as though they happened naturally in the sun but actually take all day in the hairdressers, are definitely OK now. No mistaking their source though – they are now universally known as Di-lights.

The Princess loves sailor-style outfits – very Deauville in the 'twenties'. Many are designed for her by David Sassoon, of the Belville Sassoon partnership, who was one of her first designers. His was the jolly red and white nautical-style outfit that she chose for Prince William's photographic debut (above). Softer, dressmaker versions of the sailor look, in softer pastel colours, were chosen for the Australian Tour.

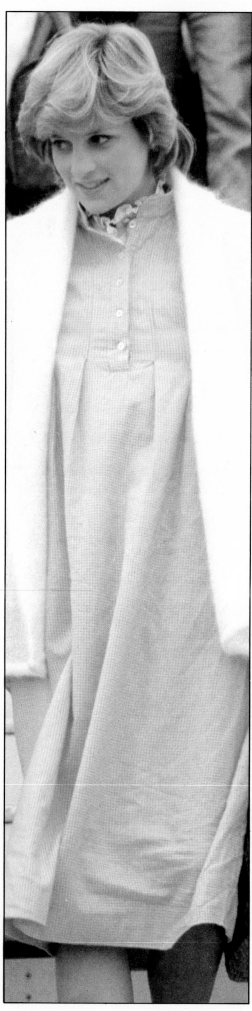

While the Royal Family traditionally choose bright colours for their clothes so that they can be spotted from afar, Diana has also shown a penchant for pastels, particularly on less formal occasions. Baby blues and pinks were a favourite and flattering choice in the last days of pregnancy, when they were often partnered by baby-soft, white angora cardigans for warmth on the polo field. Paler tones, especially white, appeared constantly Down Under, to play up the tan that the Princess quickly acquired in the blazing sun.

The Princess has admitted publicly that her favourite way of keeping warm is to wear thermal underwear from the Yorkshire firm of Damart. It means that she can get away with pretty printed silk outfits on all but the coldest days. But Royal walkabouts can be a chilly business, particularly in the depths of winter. And so for the coldest days she chooses colourful, light-weight mohair coats or the closer-fitting, formal shapes, like the military-style grey coat (left) with its black velvet trim and buttons.

It's the common touch that has especially endeared Diana to the public. Like the girl next door, she buys many of her young, casual clothes from high-street chain stores. And she wears them just as stylishly as she does those magnificent ballgowns with their designer labels. In her kindergarten days (above) she loved separates and comfortable, easy dresses, often in flower-printed Tana lawn bought from Liberty. For Balmoral she chooses suitably Scottish tweeds (as right on her honeymoon) and tartans. She even managed to look relaxed and ravishing in a huge pink maternity tent dress, its sleeves rolled up, just five days before the birth of Prince William. Another very appealing touch is the way she wears her husband's watch side by side with her own while he plays polo (above right). Chameleon-like, she's learnt very quickly to dress absolutely correctly for an enormous number and variety of occasions, but fashion experts often comment that it is in these young, casual clothes that she looks her very best.

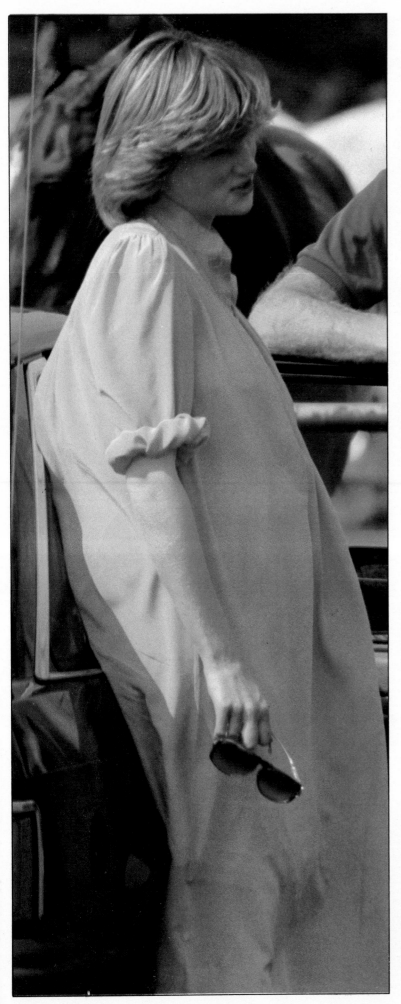

Whatever Diana's personal favourite when it comes to colour (and rumour has it that it's pink), she knows how important it is to ring the changes when constantly in the public eye. Green may not currently be a top fashion colour but it's an apt choice for a Princess of Wales, and she diplomatically chose it for her first visit to Wales (above and facing page).

On the hottest days of the Royal Tours to Australia and Canada, pretty printed silks were a cool choice, whether it was the grey and white two-piece with its pleated skirt worn on a walkabout in Ottawa, or something comfortable like the grey checked dress trimmed with yellow that was chosen for travelling with Prince William when he made his debut in Melbourne.

Stripes are high fashion and the Princess knows that latching onto a new look in its early days gives you the longest run for your money! She first wore her stunning red jerkin suit with its striped shirt for her very first visit to Ascot (right) just before the Royal Wedding, but was happy to bring it out again for the Australian Tour in April (facing page, bottom left). In between times she has worn stripes on everything from maternity dresses (for an optical slimming effect) to a favourite quilted cotton jacket, and for many silk suits and dresses.

The Princess quite obviously has a passion for pink – particularly a zinging rose pink. She's chosen it for everything from a cosy mohair worn during pregnancy to the pretty, flower-printed dress which she wore for Prince William's christening (below), proving that it's a versatile shade that looks as good in the depths of winter as it does in bright sunlight. It's not a colour that everyone can wear with such ease, but having a perfect English rose complexion helps enormously. Her soft, natural-looking make-up that suits pink so well is something that the Princess has learnt to do with the expert help of top make-up artist Barbara Daly and looks far subtler than hard matching tones. The rose pink sailor dress (facing page, top left) is the one which, quite unjustly, won her a place on some mad American's worst-dressed list. He termed it her "Mack Sennett" look.

Traditionally, royals usually wear small brimmed hats so that the public can easily see their faces. But Diana often sports something bigger, especially when she's wearing a sleeker and more sophisticated outfit; matelot shapes, for instance, like the pretty pink one on the left, or jaunty, broad-brimmed trilbies or boaters (opposite). But however broad her brim, she always manages to tip it at an angle that doesn't obscure her smile.

Ever since that very first glimpse of Diana on her wedding day, she has lived up to the world's image of her as the fairytale princess – an image deliberately created for her by the designers of that dress; the Emanuels. The shy, teenage nursery school teacher had taken just a few short months to blossom into the real-live version of the dream princess. She has lived-out the world's fantasy of how a princess should look, in an array of fabulous fairytale dresses like the beribboned and glitter-embroidered number (above right). Designed by David Sassoon it was first seen at the opening of the Gonzaga exhibition, standing out especially as all around were still wearing black – a fashion she had started with that first famous strapless black ballgown just a few months earlier. The Sassoon dress, an obvious favourite, has appeared several times since. Diana's other favourite evening-dress designers are Bruce Oldfield, Murray Arbeid, and Victor Edelstein; and she has recently revisited the Emanuels too.

That fairytale wedding dress that set the mood for how we expect our Princess to look for the grand event. David Emanuel, who designed it together with wife Elizabeth, is Welsh so it was an apt choice for the Princess of Wales. It was the Emanuel team, too, that designed the sequined chiffon dress of palest blue (top).

Sombre colours like black or grey can be difficult for a young girl to wear, but there are occasions when Diana will have to wear black, and there are signs that she likes to anyway – remember that first fantastic, strapless Emanuel ballgown? In the Autumn of 1981 Diana had all wearing capes again, and hers, in black velvet (far right), was a warm choice to cover up a green taffeta dress (plus emeralds) for a concert in Wales. Black and white was the big fashion theme for the summer of '83, and certainly one that Diana didn't miss out on. She wore her fashionable black and white print suit in New Zealand, where she was also seen in the white trilby with its wide, black satin banding.

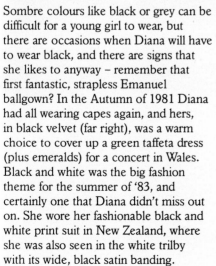

Black was a necessary choice when Diana represented the Queen at Princess Grace's funeral (above). And suitably serene and stunning she looked too, in her severe black dress quickly made up for her by Jasper Conran. Diana paired it with a simple veiled boater, which set off beautifully her dazzling diamond necklace. Black too, of course, for the Festival of Remembrance at the Albert Hall and the next day's service, although on both occasions the bright red poppy provided a splash of colour. Then there was that black velvet cape (far left) that Diana made so famous, worn in Canada over a white dress this time.

The Princess knows the power of white as an accessory colour. White collars, either crisp or frilly, have long been her hallmark, and now she adds white hats too. It's a wonderful colour for setting off a good skin; a trick that she learnt a long time ago. This includes her favourite jewellery; her various necklaces of creamy-white pearls.

Diana's jewels are already legendary. As well as having the use of the Spencer family jewels, she has quickly built up an enviable collection of her own. There is the tiara, for instance, that was a gift from the Queen, seen worn here in Canada with its nineteen little dangling pearl drops and its diamond lover's knots, and originally part of Queen Mary's collection.

The recent royal tours proved beyond doubt that our Princess of Wales is the best fashion ambassadress we could wish for. With around three changes of clothes daily on each of those hectic, non-stop schedules, it was rather like watching a one girl fashion show as these varied outfits, all worn on the Canadian Tour, demonstrate.

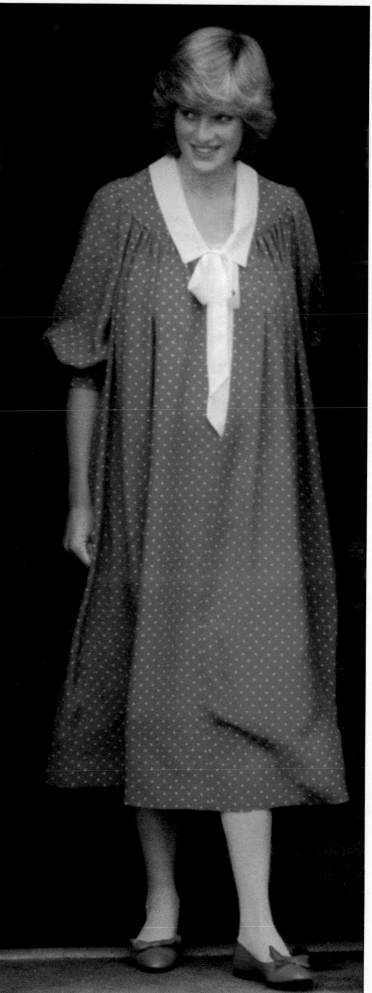

Diana has made spots almost as fashionable as stripes, and both have won a big place in her wardrobe. She found pin-sized dots particularly useful during pregnancy when they provided the ideal way of breaking up a large expanse of bright colour and were far more flattering than a distorting or enlarging print. The green dress with the white collar (facing page) was worn on leaving hospital after the birth of Prince William.

Many a shoulder has been fashionably bared since Diana first daringly revealed hers, in that strapless black taffeta ballgown worn shortly after the engagement was announced. Prince Charles quite obviously adored her in it – and so did the rag trade who copied it endlessly. Lately, she has favoured the one-shouldered look, first wearing it at the Birthright fashion show in December 1982 (above and facing page). A Bruce Oldfield design in bright blue with a silver print and Hawaiian lei effect, its softer, slimline look was to herald the demise of the ballgown. Star of the Australian Tour was the even slinkier, sexier number in silver and white, by the London based Japanese designer Hachi. Slimline too, the rose pink dress of tucked organza with shoulder bows, by Victor Edelstein, again worn in Australia.

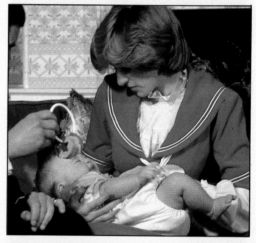

Holding the baby means clothes that will take crumpling and creasing plus the occasional dribble! And when it comes to family portraits, Diana certainly knows from experience that pretty necklines and clever collars work well, and are especially important when most of you is obscured by an armful of baby! Spotted green silk was her choice for the first picture as a new mother (left) and again, for William's New Zealand picture session (facing page, left).

Tartan is yet another old-time favourite that Diana has brought back into fashion. In fact she often chooses tartan for visits to Scotland, just as she wears red and green for Welsh visits. Critics of her expenditure on clothes should note that this outfit (right) by Caroline Charles was first seen two years ago but reappeared again recently looking just as good. To complete her tartan look in true Scottish fashion, Diana often adds a jaunty regimental-style cap (above) or a black velvet tam-o'-shanter (above right).

Diana didn't drastically alter the way she dressed to accommodate her pregnancy, and she capitalized on certain fashion features that she's made her mark. Pretty collars, for instance, either ruffled or bow-necked, are something she's always loved and worn a lot, and they worked wonders in distracting from the bulk! So did her famous pearl chokers, while stripes slimmed and spots broke up an expanse of colour. And her favourite low-heeled shoes were, of course, just right. The only thing she changed were the colours she wore, which became notably softer and more pastel in tone as pregnancy progressed.

Princess Diana's first royal tour was undoubtedly a sartorial success despite a few remarks from the Australian Press. And what other twenty-one year old could have coped with such a heavy programme of duties – up to three public appearances a day? Packing for each stopover on the tour meant packing clothes to cover this wide range of events, and it is reported that a total of fifty outfits were worn over a period of 42 days – almost every one of them with a British label! By day, she was the typical English rose in neat shapely suits with small matching hats like the svelte white number (this page, far left), or in contrast, the proud mum photographed informally in a spotted silk dress with a deep white collar.

Evening occasions in Australia and New Zealand were splendid affairs and the time to show off that new-found tan with pale, glittery fabrics, low décolleté necklines and sparkling jewels. Most sensational of all was the one-shoulder silver spangled white dress by Hachi which she wore on her last night in Melbourne (centre left). Then there was the pretty pink ruffled style (below left) from the Chelsea Design Company, and the silver threaded blue of the ruffled Bruce Oldfield dress (below). Also by Bruce, the scarlet ballgown.

Sunshine colours won the day on the Royal Tour of Australia. A ruffled suit in pale primrose yellow was a brave choice in which to face the New Zealand rain (right and facing page, bottom right). A suit with a cosily quilted jacket was warmer, and worn for a trip by tribal canoe to Waitangi (facing page, top right), while sunshine yellow made the dress worn for dinner at Government House Canberra. In silk taffeta with leg-of-mutton sleeves, this Murray Arbeid dress was teamed with the Spencer family tiara and a diamond and sapphire necklace. And for the Sunshine Plantation the choice was a yellow dress by Jan Vanvelden.

One of Diana's most unusual winter coats was the colourful basket weave number with fringed hem and neckline. The bright blue, veiled and plumed bowler was matched with handbag and shoes. Cosy coats such as these were to provide her with some good winter camouflage during pregnancy, and the bright colours must have been particularly cheering during those months of morning sickness. Another favourite during pregnancy was the rose-pink wool coat (above centre), with its frilled collar and yoke, again worn with a matching bowler; but Diana realised that plumes and veils might have been just too much with this one and settled for a simple, flat bow beneath the brim instead. One of her most successful winter outfits has been the pale banana-yellow suit trimmed and stitched with dark brown by the Sloane Ranger's newest discovery: the young Arabella Pollen.

That famous streaked bob of hair with its heavy fringe has been grown slowly and subtly longer since honeymoon days (opposite page, left). Keith Shanley of Headlines, the Kensington hairdressers, who has cared for the Princess' hair since her Sloane Ranger days (and now keeps an eye on her husband's too) is very aware that tiny hats like the pretty pink one (facing page, right) will sit more securely on longer locks. And brimmed hats like the red one (above) look all the better with a little more hair on show. Quite how much Diana's hair has grown is obvious from the contrast between the honeymoon picture (facing page, left) and the photograph taken shortly after the birth of William. The fringe now flicks up noticeably to one side for a more elegant and sophisticated effect, while the side view of Diana on tour in Australia (facing page, bottom right) shows that it is now very much longer at the back too.

Yes, Diana does go in for longish hemlines, whatever the whims of fashion, but not because she's dowdy, as the Australian papers would have it. Her legs are lovely, but she's realised that the discrepancy in height between herself and Charles can be cleverly disguised when they're photographed together if she's wearing a mid-calf length skirt which enables her to stoop slightly.

Much of Diana's popularity must be due to the fact that she is very much a Princess of the people. She's never too busy to have a chat with her audience, especially if they are children, and this is said to be another reason for her longish hemlines. Mid-calf lengths are definitely more ladylike for someone who spends so much time bending down or stooping to talk to the youngsters.

Diana's jewel box may be getting bigger by the minute, but she keeps the big gems for the biggest occasions. They certainly got a good airing in the Royal Tours of Australia at all those formal dinners. The Spencer family tiara (above and right) appeared several times. So did the huge sapphire pendant on its diamond necklace (above right) which was a wedding present, together with matching earrings and bracelet, from the Saudi Royal Family. Sapphires are very much her taste in jewellery it seems, as her choice of much-copied engagement ring illustrates. She is, of course, particularly fond of pearls and much of the credit for their recent return to fashion must be due to Diana. Not since Queen Mary's day have pearl chokers been so much in fashion, although the Princess is just as often seen wearing a simple single strand as she does here with her pink evening dress (facing page, left). But sometimes she will even wear her famous ruby and diamond drop earrings with a casual cardigan.

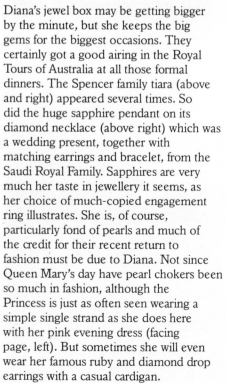

The tiara that the Queen gave to her daughter-in-law is a real dazzler: it has umpteen pearl drops and diamond lover's knots and Diana wears it on all the grandest occasions together with some very pretty pearl drop earrings with diamonds. Both did sterling duty on the Canadian Tour, looking as good with cream satin as they did with shocking pink or bright blue.

Copies of Diana's pearls, in all their many variations, have been a gift to the costume jewellery manufacturers and an absolute sell-out in the department stores.

In the Autumn of 1982, just a few months after the birth of Prince William, rumours were rife that the Princess was suffering from the slimmers' disease Anorexia Nervosa. The public, who had been used to the image of, first, the plump teenager of her engagement days (above) and then the comely bride who quickly became pregnant, were shattered to see their Princess growing thinner by the minute. But like many young mothers after the birth of their first child, Diana's shock at not being able to get back into favourite clothes immediately after the birth of Prince William probably resulted in too fast and too stringent a diet. But by the time of the Australian Tour, as the pictures (left) show, she was quite obviously in radiant good health.

By the time the Princess reached Australia she needed to be healthy indeed to keep up with her hectic schedule. Not only was she radiant, but she also had that marvellous bloom that she had gained during pregnancy. And despite the proximity of the two tours, she plunged into the Canadian Tour with just as much energy and enthusiasm.

Blue-eyed blondes traditionally look beautiful in blue, and Diana is no exception. Strong blues in every shade of royal and azure have held a favourite place in her wardrobe ever since that first engagement-day suit. And two of her greatest fashion successes on the Australian Tour were the shapely suit in turquoise-blue silk (far right) and the ruffled and silver spangled bright blue Bruce Oldfield ballgown.

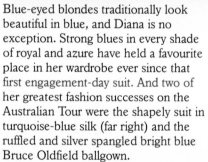

Scarlet has always been one of Diana's favourite colours. For the Canadian Tour it appeared for both formal and informal occasions, both day and night. The red suit with its slim skirt (top and facing page, top right) was purloined from

Jasper Conran's collection months ahead
of the season. Then there was the formal
red lace and taffeta dress chosen for
the farewell dinner at Government House
(above). And the dashing red and white
checked dress worn on arrival (left) as
well as the red and white spotted dress
with its matching jacket. On the
informal occasions Diana shows just how
effective a splash of red can be in
brightening up the simplest shirt and
trouser outfit.

Diana wore the cheery scarlet coat, with its deeply frilled collar, with a matching sailor hat for a visit to a Nativity play at Guildford Cathedral during pregnancy. And it is dashing outfits like these that provided inspiration for the British fashion industry at a time when there was a distinct lack of direction. Her continually-changing wardrobe has given us a choice of eye-catching styles that are both desirable and practical, young but elegant, and a welcome alternative to the baggy, tattered clothes in "distressed" fabrics stemming from the avant-garde Japanese designers.

Regal red is certainly another royal favourite and makes a princess stand out in a crowd, as Diana proved time and time again on both royal tours. Her favourite coat suit of pre-wedding days, with its co-ordinating striped blouse, came out again to do stalwart duty in Australia (facing page, far left) and there were many new red outfits too, like the Jan Vanvelden silk suit (above) with its wide, white serrated collar. It has been reported that the Princess often has something of a sense of humour when it comes to fashion; if so she may well have deliberately planned to meet the Canadian Mountie (left) in an exactly matching red; this time the tailored seven-eighths-length coat and skirt by Jasper Conran.

Another Jasper Conran suit became a favourite outfit of the Canadian Tour – this one a white suit with a long, slimline jacket. But the arrogant Jasper was quoted as disapproving of the hats the Princess puts with his clothes. Certainly this suit looks far better worn plain and uncluttered (top) than with the rather over-fussy, frilly white blouse (right) which hides its clear-cut neckline. And Diana seems to be developing a taste for more tailored lines. (Above) the cream and beige striped silk outfit worn in Australia.

Even her dresses are developing a sleeker, more slimline look along the lines of the white suit and its narrow, pencil skirt (above). The two more tailored dresses pictured here were both worn on the Canadian Tour.

Four pictures that show just how cleverly that famous hairstyle has evolved into a longer, more sophisticated look that provides the perfect framework for a tiara. The fringe sweeps sideways these days and is flicked gently upwards. Note, too, how Diana has learnt to outline her eyes with blue kohl pencil to echo the colour of those famous sapphires.

Diana's eyes are one of her most winning features, and she knows it. Jaunty, side-perched pillboxes and eye veils play them up, and yet she somehow manages to keep them well within view even when she wears broader brimmed hats or carries umbrellas. Even that original heavy fringe of pre-marriage days was never allowed to obscure them.

Feathers were forsaken for flowers on many of the hats worn in the midsummer weather of the Canadian Tour. The cream pillbox, with its matching big rose and dotted eye veil appeared at least twice. Then there was the rather more severe, smaller, crowned style (right) with its twisted band and flower trim. Even the fancy dress outfit that Diana wore for the Klondike-style barbeque (above) was festooned with flowers.

The self-patterned white cotton dress designed by Benny Ong worn barelegged and hatless for the Ayers Rock climb at the very beginning of the Australian Tour (facing page) set the scene for a less formal style of dress that the Princess adopted Down Under. There were several soft silk dresses for instance, again many worn hatless, and many designed by Dutch-born designer Jan Vanvelden, like the turquoise and yellow dresses (second column, top and centre). There were also pretty, flower-garden prints of the sort that one might wear to an English country fete. Another flower printed favourite was the quilted cotton cardigan jacket (right). Diana owns another identical one with matching skirt in a paler colour which she also wore in Australia. By the German firm of Miss Antonette, it is one of the very few foreign garments she has been seen in.

Diana obviously loved dressing up in this fabulous period outfit, with its whaleboned bodice and ruched and tiered skirt, for the Klondike-style evening barbeque held in Edmonton towards the end of the Royal Tour of Canada. For someone who loves clothes as much as she does it's a rare treat to don bustle, train and buttoned boots.

The Princess' new taste for more tailored, slimline clothes along rather more classic lines was first seen in December 1982, when she opened the Charlie Chaplin playground in London wearing the chic red coat with black revers seen opposite. And it's a taste that's developing, with several more sleek, tailored outfits like the scarlet coat and skirt (below right) and the royal blue coat dress (below and right).

Diana's hats have become noticeably less fussy of late. Many are trimmed with a simple wide band of ribbon – particularly stunning in white with a wide black satin ribbon (top centre). It's a look that is far better suited to tailored, classic clothes, although even the pale grey and white print dress worn in Canada (above) was teamed with a simple ribbon-banded grey straw hat. Diana will often wear plain white or black hats with bright colours these days and finds them versatile accessory colours on a long tour.

More dazzling gems from the Royal jewel
box. Diana may be happy to wear the same
dress twice, as here, but the jewels are
often different ones as she constantly
adds to her collection of impressive
pieces. She had, for instance, worn her
midnight-blue velvet dress with its
deep-flounced lace collar with either
sapphires or pearls around her neck. The
bright blue Bruce Oldfield dress, with
its on-shoulder Hawaiian-style ruffles,
was worn originally to her very first
public fashion show, with one of her
famous pearl chokers. Yet another
similar blue Oldfield dress appeared in
Australia bedecked with an impressive
array of sparklers plus a wide, silver
cummerbund. The Princess' taste in
jewellery is pretty rather than punchy.
No brooches, few bracelets, but nearly
always something around that long, swan-
like neck, especially at night to suit
the bare necklines that she favours.

The impressive sunray necklace of diamonds is from Queen Mary's collection, and Diana's taste seems to run along similar lines. The Spencer family tiara that she wore for her wedding was given frequent airings Down Under (above and opposite right), as was the diamond necklace with a pendant designed in the shape of the Prince of Wales' feathers (above).

The first royal tour was a tribute indeed to the circle of young British fashion designers that Diana so patriotically supports. And in her short time as a princess she has probably cast her net far wider than any royal before her, experimenting with fashion in order to evolve a very personal style of her own.

Buckingham Palace is discreet when it comes to disclosing the sources of Diana's clothes. Possibly it is because many are bought off-the-peg (something she, with her model size figure can quite easily do) instead of being made especially for her. Off-the-peg clothes can, of course, be priced very easily, while couturiers can be trusted to be discreet about prices. It could also be because she seldom makes up her mind until the very last minute about which outfit she will wear for any particular event.

Ever since that first stunning, strapless black ballgown Diana has shown how well she can bare her shoulders. And that dress seen below both with and without its matching frilled shawl was designed by David and Elizabeth Emanuel. Then the Palace announced that it would be the Emanuels who would be making that very special wedding dress too. Another stunning strapless dress (opposite) was chosen by Diana for the E. T. premiere in December 1982. This one is by French-born designer Roland Klein, who has a shop immediately below the Emanuels' Brook Street salon.

Feathers are obviously Diana's own
personal favourite when it comes to hat
trims. They're a special signature of
her milliner John Boyd, whose hands are
frequently tinted the colour of Diana's
latest outfit, as he strives to dye the
feathers to match. Feathered hats have
consequently been the big trend at Royal
Ascot over the last two years.

More of those Jasper Conran outfits on show in Canada. Raspberry pink with a pleated skirt and long, double-breasted jacket was worn casually hatless in Montague (opposite). Shown (far left) is the long red coat and slim skirt that Diana wore on her visit to Shelburne and the jade green outfit (above centre), cut on decidedly classic lines.

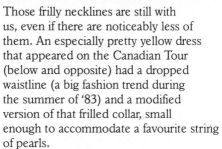

Those frilly necklines are still with us, even if there are noticeably less of them. An especially pretty yellow dress that appeared on the Canadian Tour (below and opposite) had a dropped waistline (a big fashion trend during the summer of '83) and a modified version of that frilled collar, small enough to accommodate a favourite string of pearls.

Among Diana's few imported purchases are her famous low-heeled pumps by Charles Jourdan (above right). Initially, Diana made forays into the South Molton Street boutiques to find cheaper versions, but with so much time spent on her feet she realized that there is nothing to beat the comfort of the famous French shoes.

The Princess loves babies and children and it's obvious that she's never happier or more relaxed than when there's one on hand to cuddle or charm, no matter whether it is her own or someone else's! Perhaps that's why she chose to be pictured with a toddler on each hip for those very first pre-engagement shots taken at the Young England kindergarten, when photographs (and photographers) were obviously still something of a gruelling experience for her. It explains, too, why she chooses longer length skirts much of the time. They enable her to stoop and talk to small children yet still look ladylike, and it also explains why she chooses non-crush fabrics, anti-dribble prints, and likes shapes that aren't too tight.

The Princess may be mad about clothes but once she's out on parade she likes to forget them completely and concentrate on the people she's meeting. Her handbags are almost always simple clutch shapes that she can tuck under one arm, enabling her to shake hands and collect countless posies of flowers, not to mention toys for Prince William.

While her favourite hairdresser, Kevin Shanley of Headlines, is often in tow, once the Princess is at an engagement and the wind blows, she's on her own. That's where a hat (and a spare hand) often comes in very useful! And often the flowers are so profuse that they keep both hands busy in any case.

When Diana first wore her emerald green taffeta dress (for an early pre-wedding Snowdon portrait) the emeralds were on loan from Mayfair jewellers Collingwood. Now she has a handsome diamond and emerald choker of her own, plus matching earrings (opposite). The dress, by Graham Wren of Nettie Vogues, was one of her first early off-the-peg successes – she simply spotted it in the window of Harvey Nichols' Knightsbridge store. Jewel colours, too, are the choice for many of her most stunning ballgowns.

The transition from plump young teenager to slim and sophisticated princess has been a rapid one. Diana lost a lot of weight just before the wedding day, as the picture (right) shows, and again after the birth of her baby, when she was able to wear the same dress for the Australian Tour (opposite).

The birth of Prince William gave Diana a poise she hadn't had before. At the Christening, the twenty-year-old mother showed how deftly and expertly she could already cope with her crying infant, even in front of the world's cameras. She's quite obviously a born mother and motherhood, in its turn, has given her the confidence to cope with her demanding round of public engagements.

How many young wives could cope with the strenuous round of formal engagements that Diana has taken on and which she handles like a real professional? What is more, she always looks as though she is enjoying herself. Less than two years after she married into the Royal Family she was coping magnificently with two demanding royal tours in close proximity, as these pictures, all taken on the Canadian Tour, illustrate.

Not since the White House days of Jackie Kennedy have so many pillbox-style hats been copied and worn, all thanks to Diana. She has them in all fabrics, in a selection of colours to match all her outfits. Sometimes they're decorated with matching plumes or flowers or huge bows or veils. And often when she finds a hat shape she particularly likes she will have it interpreted in lots of different colours and fabrics, like the tiny, veiled skullcap of azure blue silk which she wore in Australia (opposite). The same style appeared in acid yellow to match a yellow silk suit worn later in New Zealand. And in Canada, the pale-grey pillbox with the big, flat side bow turned up too, in an alternative cream and beige version.

A young Dutchman called Jan Vanvelden is one of the most recent designers to be called to the court of Princess Diana, and quite a number of his outfits appeared on the Australian Tour. His signature seems to be big, white serrated collars that the Princess loves and that decorated the red dress (opposite), the green spot silk dress (below centre), and was also seen in a turquoise version (above).

Diana's jewel-coloured velvet suits, with their short, shapely jackets and long, full skirts, are exactly right for late day events in autumn and winter. The bottle green suit, with its matching mini bowler, was a special choice for her first official visit to Wales. She also likes jewel colours like garnet and sapphire which look especially glowing in velvet. But the frilly white collars that she made so famous (left) are less frequent these days, and when she switched on the Regent Street lights two years ago she chose a far simpler tie-necked blouse to complement her chic Chanel-style velvet suit.

What other girl of Diana's age has to dress up so formally for so much of the time? Gradually, the Princess is evolving a certain style of her own, plus an entourage of enthusiastic and talented young designers to interpret it. Dressy, occasion clothes such as these, are what British designers are best-known for, and Diana generally makes a determined effort to buy British, thus supporting the home fashion industry.

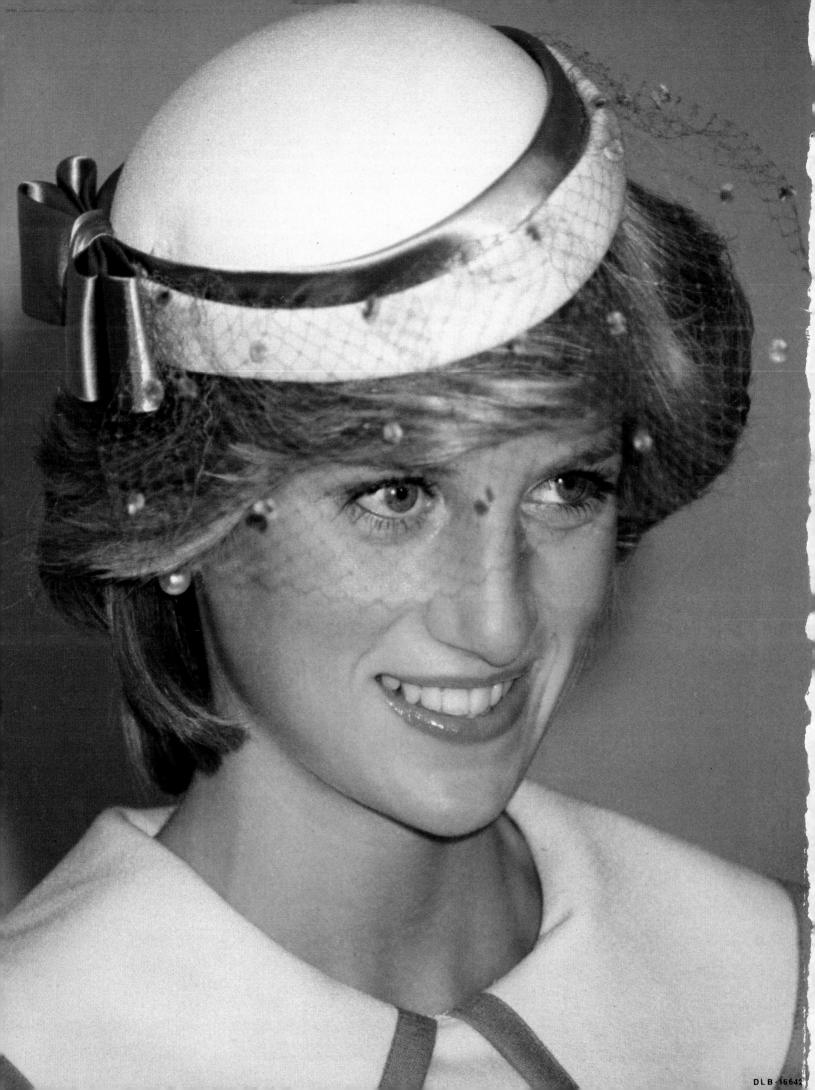